STEAM'S LAMENT
Stanier & Ivatt Pacifics

Kevin Derrick

Strathwood

STEAM'S LAMENT
Stanier & Ivatt Pacifics

First published 2022
ISBN 978-1-913390-31-0

All rights reserved. No part of this book may be reproduced or transmitted in any form or by any means, electronic or mechanical, including photocopying, recording or by any information storage and retrieval system, without written permission from the Publisher in writing.

Copyright Strathwood Publishing 2022
Published by Strathwood Publishing,
4 Shuttleworth Road,
Elm Farm Industrial Estate,
Bedford MK41 0EP
Telephone: 01234 328792
Printed by Akcent Media, Ltd.
www.strathwood.co.uk

Contents	Page
Prototype Lizzies	4
The Fateful Turbomotive	12
Loyal Service	16
Coronation Splendour	41

Prototype Lizzies

The first built of these fine Stanier Pacifics 46200 The Princess Royal climbs away from Halton Junction during 1949 with an up express from Liverpool. At this point she carries an 8A Edge Hill shed allocation plate and is in a hybrid black livery carried across from her LMS days with a modest repaint around the cab to show her new number, likewise the previous LMS smokebox numberplate as 6200 has given way too. By the time of the fine nameplate photograph opposite on 23 June 1960, 46200 had been in the attractive British Railways' version of crimson lake livery almost mimicking the earlier LMS livery since May 1958, a livery she would carry until withdrawn on 17 November 1962. **Photos:** *R.A. Whitfield/Rail Photoprints & Colour Rail*

This almost profile view on Camden's turntable in 1958 shows the recently applied lined red livery to advantage. There were to be many detail changes during the careers of these Pacifics involving tenders, boilers, fireboxes, and liveries. Needless to say, the first two built would see the most of these changes. When new as 6200 in 1933 she appeared with round buffers, a combined top feed and domed boiler along with a Fowler style of tender carrying nine tons of coal and 4,000 gallons of water. In addition, the nameplate was blank, as the locomotive was put on show at Euston in a lined grey livery in the early summer of 1933. Those early changes came fast as after all the first two locomotives were prototypes for what was to follow. The improvements were swiftly made as required, and the first two locomotives by now in a lined LMS red livery settled in on non-stop runs from Euston to Glasgow gaining the LMS much kudos against their rivals on the ECML. *Neville Stead Collection/The Transport Library*

Not so long to go for this now Carlisle Kingmoor allocated engine as 46200 The Princess Royal gracefully glides through Gleneagles with the 4:45pm fish train from Perth in the summer of 1962. *W.J. Verden Anderson/Rail Archive*

Going well as she climbs hard out of Euston and up the bank past Camden with the early evening 5:05pm express for Blackpool during 1950, we find 46201 Princess Elizabeth. Likewise, she had also ended her time with the LMS in a black livery but was now wearing a lined black livery in the same style later adopted as the standard mixed traffic livery complete with a large version of the new lion and dartboard emblem. Entering service in November 1933 she would go through fourteen changes of boiler and firebox combinations during her working career, variously with numerous variations. Her prototype sister The Princess Royal going through three fewer such changes. Three types of tender were fitted, both the prototypes began with Fowler style 4,000-gallon water capacity and 9-tons of coal on a longer than then standard fifteen-foot wheelbase, they were also wider than those previously built. Three such tenders were constructed to suit 6200-6203. Very soon it was felt that the coal capacity should be increased for the full Euston to Glasgow run, but not until both 6200 and 6201 had been tried on short spells with Stanier designed 9-ton coal capacity tenders similar to those fitted to the Jubilees then also in production, but these three enjoyed roller bearings. As 6202 was not yet completed it was decided to send the spare tender out to the USA for The Royal Scot's American tour instead to cope with the extra expected mileage it would be faced with. These three tenders were themselves prototypes as it appears they did not behave well in service with complaints that the self-trimming coal feature did not work very well and that there should be better ways to stow the fireirons and tools. All three of these tenders would soon be rebuilt and a new standard 10-ton riveted design for the whole class save for 6202 was put into service from the middle of 1936.
F.R Hebron/Rail Archive Stephenson

Opposite: This un-dated view shows 46201 Princess Elizabeth having no troubles at all as she steams nicely past the summit board at Shap, taken some time after her overhaul in May 1952 when she was released in the then standard lined green livery with the larger early emblem on her tender. This would be changed to the later style during one of her four separate visits to Crewe Works for attention during 1957. **Neville Stead Collection/The Transport Library**

The full splendour of 46201 Princess Elizabeth can be admired in this view as she descends Beattock with the up Mid-day Scot bound for Euston on 18 July 1959. At this point she was back allocated to 66A Polmadie in Glasgow, having been allocated variously to Camden, Longsight, Crewe North, and Edge Hill since leaving Polmadie a few weeks before the outbreak of war in 1939. Her best year for mileage was to be in 1936 with 83,320 to her credit. But 1961 showed a mere 2,569 as she spent most of her time in storage thanks to the arrival of the new English Electric Type 4 locomotives, later known as Class 40. Their entry into service was not without problems so the old guard came back out to do their bit, with 23,089 miles to be added to her service record during 1962, by which time over 1,147,323 miles had been run at her withdrawal on 20 October 1962. Thankfully, she was purchased for preservation on 13 February the following year. *Rail Photoprints*

In early June 1961, the driver of 46201 Princess Elizabeth brings her through the cutting just to the south of Gleneagles with the late afternoon fully fitted fish train bound for the English border and beyond.
W.J. Verden Anderson/Rail Archive Stephenson

The Fateful Turbomotive

The first two Princess Royal locomotives built under Stanier's guidance in 1935 were themselves new concepts as Pacifics for the LMS with much of their designer's features perhaps brought with him from his days at the rival GWR's 4-6-0s. The first two were built as four-cylinder locomotives, but the third was to be a brave new venture indeed. The theory of using one of the experimental Metropolitan Vickers steam turbine drive units instead suggested it might bring ultimately many advantages, such as reducing the hammer blows to the track, combined with greater power, improved fuel efficiency along with reduced running costs. It would turn out that with all of the increased construction costs together with it always being a one-of-a-kind locomotive, thus requiring specialised spares and knowledge for both driving it and for her ongoing maintenance she was doomed to be a failure. Here in her British Railways lined black guise as 46202 she sits awaiting attention yet again at Crewe Works, most likely for the last time before her rebuild to a conventional locomotive which was begun in May 1950. *Neville Stead Collection/The Transport Library*

Seen from the other side of the locomotive this time out in revenue traffic for once on one of its usual duties on the Liverpool to London route at Sutton Weaver most likely during 1949. The smaller cowlings on this side complete with a slot that looks like it should take a key as giant clockwork toy, these in fact hide the much smaller reversing turbine. When new in 1935 the cowling on this side was much shorter, the turbine failed incredibly early on in its career thus the change was made some time during the war. Likewise, the smoke deflectors were fitted later during 1939. On 1 January 1948, 6202 was once again in Crewe Works for repairs upon the nationalisation of British Railways as just one of seven such visits before her rebuilding began in 1950. Based at Camden the locomotive was further restricted by the availability of engine crews familiar with driving her and for a trained fitter to accompany her duties, in case of failure. As a result, of this and her smaller 9-ton coal capacity she was kept on the Liverpool route. All of these issues aside when working properly she was a fine machine it seems. Certainly, a more worthwhile experiment to further the development of the steam locomotive perhaps than the likes of Fowler's Fury, Gresley's Hush Hush or Bulleid's Leader. **R.A. *Whitfield/Rail Photoprints***

The rebuilding work into a conventional 4-cylinder locomotive took until 15 August 1952, it was delayed being a one-off job, but still more economic than building an extra Britannia Pacific as a replacement perhaps. Once rebuilt she carried lined green livery and was named as Princess Anne after the newly crowned Queen Elizabeth's young daughter. Here we see her ready for service once more, fresh from her rebuild at Crewe during a party visit to the works that August. Tragically she was to be involved in the Harrow disaster along with 46242 City of Glasgow and 45637 Windward Islands on 8 October 1952 just a few weeks later. Afterwards the wreck remained at Harrow unable to be moved until 13 November when it was hauled by an 8F to Crewe for assessment, it had only run 11,443 miles since its expensive rebuild. A final decision to scrap what was not salvageable from her in Crewe Works was finally made in May 1954. *Both: Kenneth Field/Rail Archive Stephenson*

Construction of the production batch of Princess Royal Pacifics at Crewe Works saw 6203 released to service on 1 July 1935, named as Princess Margaret Rose. Upon nationalisation she was only just a few weeks back into service after a heavy general overhaul in lined LMS black livery, hence her appearance in this hybrid liveried version on her home shed at Edge Hill on 17 June 1948. Her next livery variation in the British Railways' era would be into the short-lived lined blue scheme in May 1951, which in turn saw her again ex-works soon after in March 1952 in the standardised lined green seen opposite. *The Transport Treasury*

With her cylinder drain cocks open 46203 Princess Margaret Rose still looking very respectable after her recent visit to Crewe Works puts on a show at Carstairs on 22 July 1952, now based out of 66A Polmadie. Mileage pre-war for her was prolific averaging almost 7,000 miles per month, her best year being in 1936 attaining 95,476 miles. By 1952 that figure had fallen to 59,619 miles, itself a figure she would not reach again. As her more powerful brethren in the shape of Coronations held court through the 1950s along the WCML. *The Transport Treasury*

One visitor to Crewe North shed on 20 August 1955 captured this view looking up towards the double line nameplate. By now she had left 66A Polmadie first for 8A Edge Hill for just one week in May 1953 before joining the fold here at Crewe North from 23 May 1953. Her next move in September 1958 would take her back to Merseyside and Edge Hill where we see her blowing off impatiently, coaled, and ready for duty around 1960. In between she also enjoyed a brief spell based in the smoke at Camden, but the end was in sight, as every month new English Electric Type 4s were arriving on the London Midland and Scottish Regions. Carnforth shed would see her allocated there next in early 1961 as lesser duties became the norm for her and her sisters from now on. In fact, she shuffled between Crewe North, Carnforth, and both Carlisle's Upperby and Kingmoor as each tried to find her work during her last few years of service. Finally withdrawn on 20 October 1962, she was sold to Butlin's in April 1963 as a feature for the holiday camp at Pwllheli after a cosmetic restoration at Crewe Works the following month, remaining on display here until sold on again in 1975 for further preservation at the Midland Railway Centre at Butterley.

Photos: The Transport Treasury & Jim Carter/Rail Online

Two trespassing young lads are on hand as 46204 Princess Louise is captured photographically in 1950 on a down express alongside the Oxford Canal at Brinklow. It had been renumbered in April 1948 firstly with the 10-inch LMS 1946 style numerals and a scroll and serif smokebox plate, but these had both been changed to the BR standard pattern by the time this photograph was taken. Incredibly it kept its pre-war LMS crimson lake paintwork which according to some records was not repainted into lined green until 1952, although it was fitted with a domed boiler in September 1950 taken from the Turbomotive 46202. One source suggests that 46204 was then in a plain black livery with the early lion on wheel emblem on her tender and gill sans smokebox and cabside numbers. When this boiler was changed again in 1952 during a heavy general overhaul, 46204 then certainly acquired her lined green livery. *Rail Online*

The Princess Royals spent many years working on the Liverpool to Euston expresses. Edge Hill's 46204 Princess Louise makes a stirring departure for the young onlookers as she departs from Liverpool's Lime Street station in around 1953. With this example spending almost all of its last decade working from the Liverpool shed. *Kenneth Field/Rail Archive Stephenson*

Passing Weaver Junction with an up Anglo-Scottish express in 1949 we find 46205 Princess Victoria before her return from 5A Crewe North to 8A Edge Hill which took place on 1 October that year, 1949. As 46205 was the only member of the class to be fitted with her non-standard valve gear this always made her easily identifiable from afar by the cumbersome motion bracket immediately behind her cylinders. The lined black livery with British Railways spelt out in full in a larger size than her cabside numbers was applied as part of her heavy general overhaul at Crewe Works completed in November 1948. Previous to this she had remained in LMS crimson lake throughout the war years. In September 1952 her next heavy general overhaul would see her put back into service in this lined green livery after the abandonment of the blue livery, here we see her pottering about the shed yard at Edge Hill a year or two afterwards. **Photos: *R.A. Whitfield/Rail Photoprints Collection & Michael Morant Collection***

Having just been released two days previously from Crewe Works from a light intermediate overhaul 46206 Princess Marie Louise catches our cameraman's attention as she takes water at Shrewsbury before returning to Crewe on a running-in turn on 5 May 1952. Once turned and with a single all stations local lamp in position she is being readied to work back to her 5A Crewe North home shed with a lightweight secondary passenger service. These undemanding runs down to Shrewsbury and back were a regular duty used for freshly overhauled locomotives from Crewe before they were returned to their customary and normal express passenger duties from their home sheds. Four of the Princess Royal Class were seen in the short-lived lined blue livery 46203/46206/46208 and 46210, however 46206 Princess Marie Louise was the only member of her class to have a coal-pusher tender. *Photos: R.O. Tuck/Rail Archive Stephenson & Ian Turnbull/Rail Photoprints*

Seen from the footbridge and approaching Crewe from the north during March 1955 we can enjoy the arrival of 46207 Princess Arthur of Connaught with the 2:10pm Liverpool Lime Street service for Euston. From this angle we can see the cleaners at her home shed of 8A Edge Hill have not bothered to deal with the top of the engine's lined green liveried boiler barrel, tut, tut. A young spotter is on hand at Bletchley to wonder at the same locomotive as she thunders through in September 1958, four months after her latest repaint and now into the attractive lined red livery.
S.D. Wainwright/Rail Photoprints & Colour Rail

This time it is larger cabside numbers than the lettering applied to her tender that adorns 46208 Princess Helena Victoria's lined black livery as she speeds south with an up express, as the fireman has the scoop down to pick up water from Moore troughs one day in 1949.
R.A Whitfield/Rail Photoprints

In September 1950, 46208 Princess Helena Victoria was turned out in lined blue livery which she retained until the summer of 1952 when she returned to Crewe Works for a heavy general overhaul to emerge next in lined green. Here she is on 14 April that year at the head of The Merseyside Express in the cutting at Tring. *Neville Stead Collection/The Transport Library*

Opposite: The well-presented lined green 46209 Princess Beatrice from 5A Crewe North makes a splendid sight on arrival at Perth with an overnight sleeping car express from Euston on 29 July 1952, three months after her last light classified repairs at Crewe Works.
W.J. Verden Anderson/Rail Archive Stephenson

On 2 August 1957 our cameraman stands firm as 46209 Princess Beatrice thunders through Acton Bridge with the down Mid-day Scot, after the locomotive had enjoyed a brief nine-month spell allocated to Edge Hill, she was now back covering duties at Crewe North.
S.D. Wainwright/Rail Photoprints

When photographed at Crewe North on 14 June 1948 the inner motion of 46210 Lady Patricia appears to be of interest to both the driver and foreman as she has just been released from the works after a four-day repair to rectify a problem identified since her light overhaul which had only been completed just eleven days previously. That same earlier visit had also seen some adjustment to the locomotive's numbering at least.
The Transport Treasury

Our next view shows her once again at Crewe North but now resplendent in the lined blue livery on 25 July 1952, note the newly approved style of smokebox plate has since been affixed. *The Transport Treasury*

The fireman on board 46210 Lady Patricia takes a well-earned breather as his driver pushes on with the northern ascent to Shap at Bessies Ghyll with a Glasgow to Birmingham express on 13 November 1955. Both the exhaust and the locomotive look somewhat cleaner when next seen as the same engine climbs Beattock bank with the aid of a banker on this overnight sleeping car express from Euston early one July morning in 1958.
Both: W.J. Verden Anderson/Rail Archive Stephenson

Opposite: Making a manoeuvre to turn at Shrewsbury most likely after her recent light intermediate repairs at Crewe Works in early 1952, 46211 Queen Maud would be among the last to retain her lined black livery alongside 46212 Duchess of Kent until later this year.
The Transport Treasury

Showing great confidence in both the locomotive and their ability the crew of 46211 Queen Maud on 9 October 1958 are doing well as they climb Shap unaided with sixteen on the drawbar. It was after all just twenty-seven days since her last heavy general overhaul at Crewe Works.
The Transport Treasury

The fireman is busy putting a few rounds of coal into the firebox of 46212 Duchess of Kent as they climb away from the north London suburbs through Harrow under clear signals on 10 June 1960. Her last visit for repairs at Crewe Works had already taken place when she was put back into traffic on 19 January that year after a heavy general overhaul. Withdrawn on 7 October in the following year she would return once more to Crewe Works, but this time for scrapping in April 1962. These other class members 46202/46204-46211 were also cut up at Crewe, with 46200 going to Connell's at Coatbridge, thankfully leaving us the two preserved survivors 46201 and 46203 for posterity. Our penultimate view of 46212 Duchess of Kent depicts her roaring southwards at Abington soon after her final overhaul in 1960. **Photos: Colour Rail & W.J. Verden Anderson/Rail Archive Stephenson**

Coronation Splendour

Looking back at the Lizzies with views such as this one of 46212 Duchess of Kent ready for departure from Euston in the late 1950s reminds us they were a great prelude of what Sir William Stanier would bring us next. In this volume by sticking to the period after nationalisation means that we are forced to ignore all but 46243 City of Lancaster as the sole renumbered streamliner to make it past 1948. Nonetheless we start our coverage of the Coronations with 46220 Coronation herself, seen here heading south at Weaver Junction with an impressive rake of coaches in the then new livery of plum and spilt milk most likely in the summer of 1948 soon after she was renumbered, although she still clings to her old allegiances wearing some of the LMS wartime black livery applied in 1944 to her. **Photos: Rail Online & R.A Whitfield/Rail Photoprints**

All of the class would be built at Crewe Works, with the first 6220 Coronation emerging in early June 1937 as a stunningly glamorous streamlined vision in blue with silvery grey stripes to accent her sleek lines. The onset of war in 1939 brought about issues of upkeep with all of the streamlined casing hindering every day maintenance. As an austerity measure the striking blue paintwork became a much plainer black livery in March 1944. Then followed the removal of the streamlining during November 1946 leaving just a hint to what had gone before with the distinctive sloping smokebox worn by 46220 Coronation as she is pictured on the Edinburgh-Glasgow route passing Slateford Junction with the 1:30pm Edinburgh Princes Street all stations stopping passenger service for Glasgow Central on 29 September 1956. The retention of the sloping smokebox led to enthusiasts using the term 'semis' in respect of that style of locomotive (i.e., semi streamlined). A close up of the nameplate shows at least twenty-four screws fixing it to the boiler barrel, it was not going to be pinched in a hurry or come lose at speed for sure. ***Photos: David Anderson/Rail Photoprints & Ian Turnbull/Rail Photoprints***

When the locomotive lost her streamlining she also gained those hefty looking smoke deflectors in September 1946, the sloping smoke box was finally removed in March 1957. Here she passes firstly Winwick Junction on a down parcels in April 1961 and then spews steam from her motion passing the lonely signal box at Scout Green on 17 May 1962. *Photos: Hugh Ballantyne/Rail Photoprints & Rail Online*

Opposite: A well drilled fireman has 46221 Queen Elizabeth with her safety valves just whispering as they head another long rake on the steady climb away from Euston with a down express during August 1960 past South Kenton. Unfortunately, steam is being emitted from the motion once again as 46221 Queen Elizabeth has charge of this featherweight parcels working under the control of the rather unimaginatively shaped and named Chester No.1 Signal Box, most likely just a few weeks before she was withdrawn on 8 May 1963.
Photos: John Day Collection/Rail Photoprints & Jim Carter/Rail Online

Various modifications to the locomotives were made through their careers to all of the former streamliners, one of these was to enlarge the drivers front window apertures to help with forward vision. The gap between the main running plate and the front buffer support would always be a giveaway to a former streamliner though, as here at Carlisle Citadel with 46222 Queen Mary in her lined green livery on 12 September 1957. When new, she was allocated to Camden until 29 November 1939 after which she became a Polmadie locomotive for the remainder of her life, thus making her a rarer sight south of Crewe for spotters. This undated view of her passing Wigan probably dates from 1962, the box underneath the fireman's window is for the AWS (Automatic Warning System) batteries a safety feature that came late to the class. **Photos: Colour Rail & Jim Carter/Rail Online**

Another rarity for spotters and cameramen alike south of the border was to be 46223 Princess Alice, likewise a long-term resident of 66A Polmadie. Someone has had a tin of light blue Scottish Region paint out to bling up the locomotive in this view from the mid-1950s at Carlisle Citadel, as here she waits to be put back onto a northbound working to take her back home to Glasgow once again. On another occasion around the same time 46223 Princess Alice heads south with the up Caledonian around three miles north of Shap summit at Little Strickland close to Thrimby Grange.
Photos: Neville Stead Collection/The Transport Library & W.J. Verden Anderson/Rail Archive Stephenson

The fireman will need to get his injectors on to quieten down Polmadie's 46224 Princess Alexandra before departure of this morning's Royal Scot from Glasgow Central on 14 April 1955. The boiler of this locomotive became a killer on two separate occasions due to footplatemen allowing the water level to drop below the firebox crown, thus causing high-pressure steam to explode onto to themselves. The first incident was in 1940 killing the fireman and severely burning his driver. The second in early 1948 killed the driver and left the fireman with terrible burns this time.
Neville Stead Collection/The Transport Library

Not ideal for freight duties due to their 6' 9" driving wheels but certainly powerful enough being a Class 8 locomotive, 46224 Princess Alexandra drifts solemnly past Balornock engine sheds in the Glasgow suburbs early in the 1960s. *Rail Online*

In an attempt to re-instate some of the pre-war glamour back into the new nationalised railway several of the Coronation class Pacifics joined other top-link locomotives in being turned out in a lined blue livery for a short while in the early 1950s. Among these was 46225 Duchess of Gloucester, showing herself off here ex-works at Crewe on 26 March 1950. There were to be several interpretations of these early blue liveries, starting in May 1948 with all but nine of the thirty-eight strong class wearing one the blue liveries at one time or another in BR ownership. In fact, lined blue remained on 46225 Duchess of Gloucester until going into lined green as late as January 1955. Here she is thus, arriving with the up Mid-day Scot at Carlisle on 6 June 1953. *Photos: Colour Rail & George C. Lander/Rail Photoprints*

Opposite: As one of the longer lasting and well-travelled higher mileage members of the class 46225 Duchess of Gloucester was well photographed too. Although she did have a darker side when she was derailed at Mossland on poorly maintained track on 15 May 1944, resulting in three deaths. Her fresh paintwork in August 1958 caught another photographer's attention ex-works again at Crewe this time in an attractive lined out brick red colour scheme, one of eleven so treated in another short-lived variation.
Rail Online

Her next call to Crewe Works for repairs would see 46225 Duchess of Gloucester sent back to work in a darker LMS style of crimson lake livery with less obvious lining. The ghastly yellow warning strip on the cab sides appeared before she was withdrawn as a reminder that she was supposed to venture south no longer from Crewe and to run further under the 25kv overhead wiring. This is her standing beneath the deadly high-tension wiring during August 1964 a matter of weeks before being withdrawn on 12 September. Her demise would be at the hands of the cutters active in the West of Scotland Shipbreaking Company in Troon sometime during December the same year.
Strathwood Library Collection

Another of the eight class members to meet their destruction at Troon would be 46226 Duchess of Norfolk. In happier days but sadly inclement weather we find her at Carlisle Upperby in lined blue livery somewhere between receiving her non-sloping smokebox in October 1952 and being painted into green livery in May 1954. On 23 April 1962, the fireman rides shotgun as they draw into Stirling heading south, ready for a dash to top up his water supply during the brief station stop. Passengers carrying heavy suitcases as luggage was more commonplace back then it seems.
Photos: Strathwood Library Collection & Peter Simmonds

Although a regular south of the border earlier in LMS days, now as 46227 Duchess of Devonshire would become more of a recluse photographically once transferred to 66A Polmadie after 12 June 1948. This undated view shows her sitting quietly at Edinburgh's Princes Street station wearing her lined green livery with the earlier crest between April 1953 and going into Crewe Works for a light intermediate overhaul in November 1957. After release back into service on 8 February 1958 she would then remain in the later version of lined green as seen next with her driver in conversation with some enthusiasts at Crewe North on 24 June 1961. Her last reported day in service would be during the week ending 29 December 1962 after which she would be left out in the cold during that horrid winter, first of all at 66A Polmadie, then afterwards from May until October dumped at 65C Parkhead. Whereupon she was tripped to 65A Eastfield to be prepared for her final journey south to Crewe Works in early November, pausing for a few days at 66E Carstairs en-route. Finally, she arrived at the famous railway town's 5B Crewe South shed around the 8th of the month. Next came the short journey to be tripped into the works and she was reported as scrapped completely by the 29th.

Photos: Neville Stead Collection The Transport Library & Colour Rail

The condition of 46228 Duchess of Rutland in this undated view at Carlisle Upperby suggests it was taken before its smokebox was modified during a works visit to Crewe beginning on 11 November 1953 but after August 1950 when it was repainted into lined blue, after almost three years of running in a hybrid version of LMS lined black. Another undated shot of 46228 Duchess of Rutland shows her picking up water from Dillicar troughs would have been taken post her 21 June 1958 release from Crewe Works in the British Railways style of the former LMS crimson lake livery. Withdrawal came the week ending 12 September 1964 as most of the survivors were withdrawn en-bloc, she would join eight others in being swiftly dealt with by Cashmore's at their Great Bridge premises within just four months, such was the haste to dispose of them at the time.
Photos: Rail Photoprints & The Neville Stead Collection/The Transport Library

In what might seem unlikely to some readers, 46229 Duchess of Hamilton is another rarer locomotive photographically at least during her British Railways career. In this instance it is not because she was a Scottish based locomotive at all, in fact she moved variously seven times between Crewe North, Camden, Upperby and Edge Hill sheds. Her mileage was around average too she also carried versions of most of the liveries, so what was it? She would ultimately make up for it in her preservation years of course. Our first view on the left shows her in the lines most likely on a weekend at 1A Willesden dressed in her lined green livery which she wore with the early crest from April 1952 until heading into Crewe Works in July 1958, for a heavy intermediate overhaul. This would see her out-shopped in the attractively lined out brick red scheme on 10 September 1958, this livery would however be short-lived as she was back again at Crewe on 17 August the following year for a heavy general overhaul next. This saw her final livery change into the now late in the day adopted LMS style of crimson lake for her until withdrawn the week ending 15 February 1964. Thankfully to be snapped up at the time by the South African born Sir Billy Butlin for display at his latest holiday camp at Minehead. Our second view dates from 28 April 1962, as 46229 Duchess of Hamilton has been relegated to working a Holyhead to Crewe parcels train, seen approaching Chester's No.6 Signal Box, the wagons on the line above are on the approaches to the city's Northgate station.

We should also not overlook that Duchess of Hamilton masqueraded as 6220 Coronation from January 1939 until 1943 as they exchanged identities in order that the then world record holder 6220 Coronation with a speed of 114mph could be seen on display promoting the LMS and Great Britain at the New York World's Fair. All because the real locomotive was due an overhaul and was not fit to take part herself. As part of the trip to the USA, the imposter 6220 Coronation made an extended tour of the country on display as a big promotional exercise. Events however were overtaken by the outbreak of war that September, as a result what was really 6229 Duchess of Hamilton was retained the other side of the Atlantic until repatriated safely home once again in 1943, when the locomotives regained their original identities once more. In her four-year exile in the USA the locomotive only recorded 3,120 miles of her 1,454,892 officially accredited service mileage.

Photos: Neville Stead Collection/ The Transport Library & Jim Carter/ Rail Online

The first five locomotives 6220-6224 were released as streamliners in the distinctive light blue livery during 1937, followed in 1938 by 6225-6229 once again in that extravagant style but this time in crimson lake and gold striping instead. Parallel to this second batch of Coronations arriving from Crewe Works in 1938, 6230-6234 were sent into service without any of the then fashionable streamlined casings as conventional locomotives, becoming known as the Duchess Class. Seen at her home shed 66A Polmadie in the earlier darker blue livery during 1948, 46230 Duchess of Buccleuch had gained this experimental scheme that May and would wear it until leaving Crewe Works after her next heavy general overhaul in early May 1952, when she adopted the now standardised lined green livery. It is the later style of crest that adorns her tender underneath the filth in the view opposite as she departs from Glasgow's St. Enoch station with the 5:30pm departure bound for Carlisle on 4 September 1962. In compiling this volume, we would suggest she was perhaps the least photographed member of the lot with 46252 City of Leicester running a close second. Another point of note for 46230 Duchess of Buccleuch is that she holds the record for the highest individual annual mileage for her class with the 94,114-mile run during 1956. Yet she was still so camera shy! *Photos: Michael Morant Collection & The Transport Treasury*

Another of the camera-shy rarities 46231 Duchess of Atholl shows off both her experimental darker blue livery and the reason for fitting smoke deflectors to the design as an afterthought as she starts to accelerate away from Dutton Viaduct near Weaver Junction going north around 1949. One of the other features of those locomotives built without the streamlined casing is the conventional Stanier style of curvature of the running plate down to the front buffer beam and the infill plating. Ably shown off in this view of the engine having worked south from her long-term home shed of 66A Polmadie to here at 5A Crewe North in the early sixties before heading back north once more. On 21 July 1945 as 6231 Duchess of Atholl approached Ecclefechan she was in collision with a goods setting back into the sidings, killing both of her crew, and injuring thirty-one passengers in her train. The crash was attributed to a large pall of smoke from the locomotive obscuring the signals at the time.
Photos: R.A. Whitfield/Rail Photoprints & Jim Carter/Rail Online

Another of the early experimental blue livery engines was 46232 Duchess of Montrose, here she stands at Crewe for her portrait to be captured on 22 May 1948. The first two of the class to be fitted with smoke deflectors had been 6232 Duchess of Montrose and 6252 City of Leicester in early 1945. Perhaps the tragic incident of 6231 Duchess of Buccleuch at Ecclefechan forced the decision home and all the class had been fitted with them by 1949. A near tragedy involving 6232 Duchess of Montrose, was fortunately avoided on 16 November 1940 when she collided with girders from the recently bombed Rose Lane bridge at Berkhamsted. There were no serious injuries except to the locomotive which was put of action for thirty-eight days for repairs at Crewe. *Colour Rail*

Footplate crews are seen busy preparing their steeds for the road in this view taken at Carlisle Kingmoor on 21 May 1952. At this point 46232 Duchess of Montrose had been just six-months since her previous heavy general overhaul at Crewe. Part of which saw her sent out in what would become the standardised lined green livery for all express steam locomotives for the next few years at least, as such she was the first of her class to be so treated in November 1951, the next to follow would be 46252 City of Leicester at the end of January 1952. **Neville Stead Collection/The Transport Library**

Although she bears a proud Scottish name, 46233 Duchess of Sutherland was always allocated in her service days to engine sheds south of the border. That said here she is posed nicely at 66A Polmadie ready to head The Mid-day Scot on this morning in the mid-fifties. Although she spent two separate prolonged periods in storage during the winters of both 1962 and 1963, she still managed above average mileage for her class of 1,644,071 on her record card when she was withdrawn the week ending 8 February 1964. *Rail Online*

On a sunny mid-winters day in early 1961 others are on hand to watch the driver of 46233 Duchess of Sutherland who was by now an 8A Edge Hill allocated locomotive reversing back onto the shed at Camden. After most likely arriving in the capital on a Liverpool express and having already passed the shed an hour or so earlier with her train. Little would they know she would within a few short years be mounted as an exhibit at Butlins Holiday Camp at Ayr as her first home in preservation. *John Day Collection/Rail Photoprints*

Nicely framed 46234 Duchess of Abercorn is going well as she passes Thrimby Woods on the northern ascent to Shap around 1959.
W.J. Verden Anderson/Rail Archive Stephenson

The clean exhaust stream trailing from 46234 Duchess of Abercorn suggests her driver has it all under control as they climb past Scout Green signal box on a down train around 1961.
W.J. Verden Anderson/Rail Archive Stephenson

Two views of our final lucky class member 46235 City of Birmingham to gain a place in railway preservation. She was originally a streamliner and the first of the final batch of them from 6235-6248 once again in crimson lake livery. The first ten being built during 1939/40, then the toughest of the war years forced a gap until the middle of 1943 when the final four were constructed. Fate decreed that 46235 City of Birmingham would be the first of the streamliners to be rebuilt in conventional form in April 1946, retaining clues such as the original narrow front cab windows at first and the sloping smokebox so distinctive here ex-works in lined green for the first time at Crewe North on 16 May 1953, having just been repainted from the later version of lined blue. Comparing her with the scene opposite after she had lost her sloping smoke box in September 1956, we see her on arrival at Euston on 7 September 1962, having brought in the 8.00am express from Manchester. Withdrawn the week ending 12 September 1964, she was set aside and cosmetically restored at Crewe Works to be a prime exhibit within the Birmingham Museum of Science & Industry where she has remained ever since.
Photos: Rail Online & Brian Stephenson/Rail Online

A chance to play spot the difference with these two views of City of Bradford taken during 1948. She had only just been rebuilt without her streamlining and released from Crewe on 20 March complete with her new numbering as M6236 in a hastily approved British Railways version of the LMS lined black colour scheme. This is her on shed at Crewe North with an unknown sister soon afterwards. Being fresh from works she was to be one of the locomotives selected for the famed 1948 Locomotive Interchange Trials, as here on the approaches to Paddington with the 1.44pm arrival from Plymouth on 21 May 1948. She represented the Coronations in the express passenger category of these official trials and worked on the Southern, Western and Eastern Regions and this second picture is of the 8.30am departure from Plymouth. The locomotive performed well especially whilst here on the Western Region tackling the banks between Newton Abbot and Plymouth in both directions in style, but very nearly came to grief when on the Eastern Region. Manned by former LMS driver Brayford and his regular fireman Saint, 46236 went through the 20-m.p.h. speed restriction at the northern approach to Peterborough North station at almost 60-m.p.h. due to the driver misunderstanding an instruction to reduce speed given to him by the ex LNER driver riding with them on the footplate, but thankfully the train came to no harm. ***Photos: Rail Photoprints & F.R. Hebron/Rail Archive Stephenson***

As there were no water troughs available on the Southern it was decided to pair 46236 City of Bradford with the tender from a Riddles Austerity 2-8-0 for her runs to increase her water capacity up to 5,000 gallons from the normal 4,800 gallons available to her footplate crew. Although the authorities insisted that all locomotives in the trials had their allocated new British Railways numbers, someone saw the chance for themselves to rub LMS into their former rivals' noses by having LMS specially painted upon the Austerity's tender, even though the LMS never possessed any and this example was borrowed from the newly formed Western Region! This was the scene as 46236 City of Bradford set off from Waterloo with the Atlantic Coast Express in June 1948. *F.R. Hebron/Rail Archive Stephenson*

The later modified larger cab window aperture shows well here as 46236 City of Bradford now in lined green livery, albeit grubby, heads past the yards to the south of Carlisle at Upperby on 21 April 1954.
Neville Stead Collection/ The Transport Library

Now this is a lot of mail traffic to deal with alongside 46236 City of Bradford at Euston on 8 April 1960, no wonder the poor fellow sitting down looks resigned to a lot of humping heavy mail bags. Our award for the most photographed class member goes to 46236 City of Bradford with just behind in a close second place awarded to 46256 Sir William A Stanier F.R.S. in this view the former has today's up Royal Scot running under caution at Birdswood on 30 April a few weeks after our first view at Euston, as the gang above on the Liverpool route work towards the raising of the structure by sixteen inches for electrification. *Photos: Colour Rail & R.A. Whitfield/Rail Photoprints*

The headlamps are set to show everyone along the route that 46237 City of Bristol is today on Royal Train duty from Euston to Ballater, in her well preened lined blue livery she passes Headstone Lane one day in 1951. Then towards the end of her working life in the early sixties, 46237 City of Bristol still makes an impressive sight even in her unkempt state as she sweeps around the curves near Stafford still on the express passenger work she was originally designed for. *Photos: C.R.L. Coles/Rail Archive Stephenson & Michael Morant Collection*

Goods and parcels workings for the class were becoming more commonplace by 1964 as the English Electric Type 4 diesels now held sway on the majority of the express turns along the WCML. Here 46237 City of Bristol makes brisk progress with this fitted freight at Broughton on 26 March 1964. In her last few weeks, she wore a yellow ribbon on her cabside forbidding use south of Crewe under the wires officially. Simmering on shed at Carlisle Upperby on 30 August 1964 she was facing imminent withdrawal the week ending 12 September. *Photos: Rail Photoprints & Colour Rail*

The streamlining on 46238 City of Carlisle had been removed early in 1947 when she lost her plain black wartime colours in favour of the LMS lined black livery, which in turn morphed into this British Railways version now worn by the locomotive when seen at Crewe North on 17 July 1951. A lined green livery came next after her overhaul in February 1952, which she now carries under the grime, unaided with fifteen on, at Shap Wells a few years later. *Photos: Colour Rail & Neville Stead Collection/The Transport Library*

Opposite: Another of the class to be a regular in front of enthusiasts' cameras back in the 1950s and 1960s would be 46238 City of Carlisle, being appropriately based in her home city at Upperby from 1951 until withdrawn, that is save for a fortnight away on loan at Camden during May 1952. When she was recorded at Crewe on 26 July 1961, her lustrous crimson paintwork still reflected her recent heavy general overhaul in the nearby works, completed only three weeks beforehand. The following year her footplate crew on 24 January had a dreadful day with her and some explaining to do in front of the foreman afterwards no doubt, when they let her water level drop far enough to collapse the firebox at Bletchley. ***The Transport Treasury***

A great chance to compose this delightful photograph befell our cameraman at Tebay on 26 June 1964, as 46238 City of Carlisle had just drawn to a halt to allow the Fairburn 2-6-4T banker 42095 to buffer up ready for the push to Shap summit ahead. The fireman has time and confidence in his steed to look out and enjoy the sunshine, as he clearly has his fire and boiler in good order for the climb with this fitted parcels working in her last three months of active service.
David P. Williams/Rail Online

An unusual livery variant next as applied to 46239 City of Chester still in the LMS 1946 livery as amended by British Railways during August 1948 using the short-lived BLOCK style of numerals favoured by Crewe and Horwich works just after nationalisation, before the introduction of the Gill Sans font transfers. Although this view is both undated and without a location on the negative sleeve, we think it is from 1949 and taken appropriately alongside the WCML perhaps near Weaver Junction in Cheshire. The fireman appears to be about to fire 46239, the locomotive was shedded at 1B Camden at this time and stayed until July 1963. *Rail Online*

In another undated view of 46239 City of Chester we find her much cleaner in appearance in the lines at Crewe North. After the previous shot she gained the attractive British Railways lined blue livery which she wore from July 1950 until a switch to lined green with this earlier crest in August 1954. Thus, dating this shot between then and the next repaint with the later crest in March of 1958, a livery she would carry to the scrappers at Cashmore's of Great Bridge in December of 1964. *Neville Stead Collection/The Transport Library*

Opposite: If we compare the view opposite of 46239 City of Chester awaiting departure from Holyhead in the early summer of 1964 with the one on the previous page we can see the addition of the Automatic Warning System (AWS) which came late to the class. Also, she was clearly another example given the warning stripe for absent-minded footplatemen who would know the rules applying to them and their route cards anyway for the class.
Strathwood Library Collection

Right: The joy on this young man's face suggests this might have been the moment he cleared his Duchesses at a time when he thought he might miss out, as they were rapidly disappearing from the daily action for the platform spotters here at Preston on 7 September 1964. The rain has not put him off and indeed the locomotive was officially withdrawn five days later after working this Euston to Carlisle service, so his glee is fully justified in our view.
Horace Gamble/The Transport Library

Larger LMS style of numerals are worn by 46240 City of Coventry after her recent visit to Crewe Works during July and August of 1948. She was captured heading north past Weaver Junction the following year. After her next paint job into lined blue livery in January 1950, she looks more the part two months later on 25 March photographed being cleaned at her home shed of Camden prior to working a Grand National special to Aintree. We wonder how many of those cleaners stuck with the job to become drivers in the end.
Photos: R.A. Whitfield/Rail Photoprints & F.R. Hebron/Rail Archive Stephenson

Our next view of 46240 City of Coventry catches her in the short-lived version of lined brick red livery, one sunny day at Crewe North during July 1958. This livery replaced the lined green colour scheme that was applied after the lined blue one which was itself supposed to have been the first standardised British Railways express locomotive livery. The city's crest is proudly worn above the chromium plated nameplate on another well photographed example of the class. When built as a crimson lake streamliner in March 1940, the accountants declared her construction costs to have been £10,838 as a combined figure for both engine and tender, which seems a bargain today considering she gave over 1,685,042 of service across twenty-four years of traffic. ***Both: Colour Rail***

Positively gleaming in the sunshine on shed at 1B Camden alongside one her replacements, 46240 City of Coventry stands proudly displaying her final change of livery into the crimson lake version adopted by her as part of a last gasp heavy intermediate repair undertaken at Crewe Works during the summer of 1960. Such was the pride taken by Camden of her she was still a perfect picture in September 1962. Standards were slipping by this next view of her on the day of her transfer from 1A Willesden to here at Crewe North on 29 August 1964, just two weeks from being withdrawn as well.
Photos: Colour Rail & Strathwood Library Collection

On 20 September 1948, 1B Camden allocated 46241 City of Edinburgh thunders out of the tunnels at Kensal Green with a down express.
*Neville Stead Collection/
The Transport Library*

The freshly applied lined blue livery here on 46241 City of Edinburgh on shed at Crewe North in September/October 1949 certainly looked great. Unfortunately, the paint pigment used within it appeared not wear so well in service, hence the decision to use the dark Brunswick green instead going forward. This was no doubt very alien and a bit too Great Western in flavour for the men of Crewe and Derby who seemed to be making all of these decisions for the now nationalised railway, was the idea of blue put forward by a strong minded ex-Caledonian Railway official in the first place perhaps?
Rail Online

Camden's cleaners have clearly expended plenty of time and effort upon 46242 City of Glasgow in this scene from around 1951. Although responsible for the initial collision at Harrow and Wealdstone on 8 October 1952, 46242 although sustaining substantial damage in the tragic carnage that followed, was to be the only locomotive of the three involved that day to be rebuilt and not withdrawn. Following a year out of service and at a cost of almost seven thousand pounds it was returned to traffic almost exactly twelve months later in October 1953.
Photos: Rail Archive Stephenson & Strathwood Library Collection

Although originally one of the streamliners, after her major repairs necessitated by the Harrow crash, 46242 City of Glasgow was rebuilt with a continuous running plate in the style of the non-streamlined locomotives, as seen here with the up Caledonian near Thrimby Grange on 26 September 1958. Those repairs took just over a year to complete with the engine managing a further ten years of service life as a result she attained a very creditable final mileage of 1,555,280 miles when irrevocably taken out of traffic the week ending 19 October 1963. Then being scrapped within Crewe Works within just a few weeks later. This side profile view again shows the now curved profile as she has charge this time of the down Royal Scot one day during 1961 near Elvanfoot. Despite her name as City of Glasgow, 46242 spent much of her twenty-three-year career based south of the border with just two spells based at 66A Polmadie. **Photos: *D.M.C. Hepburne-Scott/Rail Archive Stephenson & David Anderson/Rail Photoprints***

Several publications on these flagship locomotives previously released elsewhere have shown conflicting dates for some information, such as which locomotives were actually de-streamlined before nationalisation. Evidence suggests that both 6226 Duchess of Norfolk and 46243 City of Lancaster lasted beyond the first day of January 1948 in their streamlined form in traffic. The engine card for 6226 Duchess of Norfolk gives credence that she was de-streamlined as part of her heavy general overhaul at Crewe in the late summer of 1948, leaving just City of Lancaster which had been renumbered into the new British Railways format as 46243 during the week ending 24 April 1948. Here she is most likely early the following year in 1949 wearing her by now scruffy LMS wartime plain black livery at Crewe North. Her call into the works as the last to have her casing removed as part of a heavy general overhaul, begun on 1 May 1949. *W.H. Whitworth/Rail Archive Stephenson*

We move sharply now to the very end of 46243 City of Lancaster's existence with the first view taken at Carlisle Upperby just before being withdrawn in September 1964 and finally at her grave in the Central Wagon Works at Ince in July 1965.
Both: Strathwood Library Collection

The last working in streamlined condition for 6244 King George VI would unfortunately be a tragic one. The locomotive was working the 8:30am Euston to Liverpool on 21 July 1947, when it became derailed due to poor track maintenance near Polesworth in Staffordshire. As a result, five people died in the accident and the locomotive was sent to Crewe Works for repairs which saw it rebuilt and back in service that September. On the wet and dismal afternoon of 21 April 1962, 46244 King George VI blasts off northwards from Carlisle towards Glasgow. Next we catch sight of it arriving at Carstairs station on 21 September 1963 with the six coach 12:25pm (SO) Glasgow (Central) to Lockerbie stopping passenger train.
Photos: David P. Williams/Rail Online & J & J Collection/Rail Photoprints

The much photographed 46245 City of London in all her glory is next with the up Caledonian at Thrimby Grange and in close up during the late 1950s.
Photos: W.J. Verden Anderson/Rail Archive Stephenson & Colour Rail

Opposite: Resplendent in the London Midland Region's version of the former LMS crimson lake livery, 46245 City of London catches the eye nicely being prepared for duty in the sunshine at Willesden on 27 June 1964. *R.C.T.S. Collection*

She was no stranger in her latter years for use on enthusiast's specials, however by 1 September 1964 the writing was on the wall for all the survivors of the class. On this day she hauled what was booked as just another Ian Allan Rail Tour from Paddington to here at Crewe and back, seemingly just for enthusiasts to have a tour of the works. In the event it seems 46245 City of London did not enjoy the best of runs in either direction that day. Rather than visit the works some spotters preferring to bunk the shed here at Crewe North instead where we see the locomotive being turned. The route taken was via the Western Region through High Wycombe, Birmingham Snow Hill, Wolverhampton, and Shrewsbury to comply with the yellow warning stripe now adorning her cabside. It was also thought to be the locomotive's last actual run during her active service life, being withdrawn officially eleven days later. **Jim Carter/Rail Online**

The final locomotive to have her sloping smokebox replaced would be 46246 City of Manchester which took place in April/May 1960. This meant she could still be seen in this condition as a semi here at Carlisle with her newer British Railways emblem in lined green livery on 27 July 1957. A repaint into the early version of brick red livery ensued the following year during October, before being repainted once again, this time into the later version of LMS crimson lake in April/May 1960, no longer as a semi. This is her posed at Camden on 29 August 1961.
Photos: Colour Rail & Neville Stead Collection/The Transport Library

Drama as 46247 City of Liverpool takes water from Rugby troughs shortly before passing Newbold with a down express from Euston in October 1949. Still at this time wearing her hybrid nationalised version of LMS lined black livery. On 9 July 1961, she was much smarter when turned out for duty at Leeds City for the first leg of a tour around the England/Scotland borders. She had just transferred the previous month onto the books of Carlisle Kingmoor having been a Camden based locomotive since new in September 1943.
Photos: W.J. Verden Anderson/Rail Archive Stephenson & Rail Photoprints Collection

Opposite: Next comes 46248 City of Leeds herself, this view was taken during her heavy general overhaul within Crewe Works between 24 August and 1 October 1953. She would lose her lined British Railways black livery in favour of the lined green scheme by the time she was ready for a return to traffic once more.
Kenneth Field/Rail Archive Stephenson

Right: A trackside worker glances towards 46248 City of Leeds as she runs through Chester with a Holyhead to Euston service on 7 June 1962. The continued arrival of new English Electric Type 4 diesel locomotives would see this fine steam locomotive placed into store for a month before the year's end and once again during the following year from 24 September until 12 December 1963, as their duties dried up. Although she would be one of the lowest mileage examples in her class, she still managed the seventh highest average annual mileage of 70,400 miles. ***Rail Online***

Camden's 46249 City of Sheffield is far from home on 22 April 1954, as she prepares to head back southwards on today's Mid-day Scot from Glasgow Central. Soon she will lose her lined blue livery as part of her next visit to Crewe Works in just four months' time. In our next view she is the star in the middle of this line up at Carlisle Citadel around the same time period during 1954 in between 72006 Clan Mackenzie and 46123 Royal Irish Fusilier. *Both: The Transport Treasury*

Another view from almost the exact same spot at Carlisle Citadel a few years later in the summer of 1957 brings us 46250 City of Lichfield, just before she headed for Crewe Works and a repaint into the last version of lined green livery. Which is also how we see her now wearing a 12B Carlisle Upperby shed plate on shed at Shrewsbury around 1961. *Photos: Rail Photoprints & Colour Rail*

Our unknown cameraman has ventured out into the rain under the almost glass-less roof at Carlisle Citadel during 1956, in order to capture this view of 46251 City of Nottingham during her stop for passengers and to take on more water. Eight years previously on 17 April 1948 while still running as 6251, she was hauling the up-West Coast Postal just after midnight near Winsford, when she ran into the rear of the 5:40pm Glasgow to Euston hauled by 6207 Princess Arthur of Connaught. With the sad loss of twenty-four lives, the cause was a young soldier pulling the communication chord and the signalman had not seen 6207 pass his box and leave the section when bringing on the postal. A visit to 66A Polmadie on 18 April 1960 finds 46251 City of Nottingham being prepared for her next run south. **Photos: Strathwood Library Collection & J.E. Bell/The Transport Library**

The history file for 46252 City of Leicester is another one tarnished with an accident at Polesworth, this time attributed to the driver missing a signal at caution on 11 November 1951. Heading south with a Glasgow to Euston express he was signalled to take a crossover which he took with excessive speed which derailed the locomotive sending it over on its side, fortunately the tender and train's carriages stayed upright keeping casualties to a minimum. Several years after her repairs for this we see her first at Grayrigg during one of her spells based at 5A Crewe North in the mid-1950s, then ready for the off at Preston around 1961. **Neville Stead Collection/The Transport Library & The Mike Morant Collection**

The signalman has a commanding view of the scene at Preston with memories of the LNWR still being evoked all around, as 46253 City of St. Albans departs with a Glasgow Central to Euston express in August 1949. The locomotive is in LNWR style lined black also favoured post-war by the LMS and some of the carriages appear to be in the early BR experimental livery of plum and spilt milk. At this point the engine was only three years old she would not be withdrawn until the week ending 26 January 1963, after a working life of just fourteen years and four months, the third shortest of her class. *D.T. Greenwood/Rail Archive Stephenson*

Hardly a job requiring the use of an 8P power-rated Pacific as 46253 City of St. Albans canters along easily at Shap sometime between 1954 and the end of 1957 before her move to 5B Crewe North in September 1957. *Neville Stead Collection/The Transport Library*

The renumbering into the British Railways style for 46254 City of Stoke-on-Trent from her original 6254 took place the week ending 23 July 1949. This involved an exchange of smokebox number plate into the revised pattern along with repainting the cabside. Closer inspection shows the locomotive's power rating to be showing as 7P rather than 8P as they would be classified after 1951. Although this photograph of her on shed at Camden is un-dated we suspect it was taken just a few weeks after her renumbering as the cameraman recorded these changes for posterity. A full repaint into the lined blue livery would take place the following year during the engine's first heavy general overhaul at Crewe Works. *W.J. Reynolds/Rail Archive Stephenson*

Showing off her final livery variation after her light casual overhaul at Crewe in the late spring of 1960, she looks magnificent in crimson lake awaiting a recall to traffic. Sadly, her annual mileage would drop away year on year from now onwards up until being withdrawn the week ending 12 September 1964, as part of the great cull to dispose of the final class members. Rumours that they might find homes elsewhere such as on the Southern Region to Bournemouth and Weymouth were quickly squashed as they were rapidly scrapped instead, this example heading to J. Cashmore at Great Bridge for the sentence to be carried out during December 1964. ***Strathwood Library Collection***

An anomaly arises here with 46255 City of Hereford bringing the up Shamrock past Watford's deserted shed sometime after her repaint into the later lined green which had taken place in November 1957, and some time obviously before her withdrawal and the arrival of the overhead electrification masts to this part of Hertfordshire in 1964. However, she bears an 8A Edge Hill shed plate, yet the published sources all suggest she was based at Carlisle's Upperby firstly and then to Kingmoor throughout this period of which the latter is where we see her opposite dressed correctly albeit in a filthy state by 1963. *Photos: Rail Archive Stephenson & Colour Rail*

The final two locomotives were built with modifications specified by George Ivatt who succeeded the great man in office as CME of the LMS. The gratitude of the LMS was reflected by naming the penultimate locomotive 6256 as Sir William A. Stanier F.R.S., here she heads northbound at Brinklow during 1950 on The Mid-day Scot, loaded to seventeen coaches. Having entered traffic as 6256 an LMS engine in December 1947, just two weeks before nationalisation. The original 1946 style of LMS-pattern lined black livery being replaced by the British Railways version in October 1948, at the same time her electric lighting equipment was fitted. Several distinctive features of the last two locomotives are visible in the view opposite: the cut-down cab side sheets, the replacement pony truck and the part-welded tender fitted with roller bearings as shown by the circular axle-box covers. Interestingly, she also has two Smith-Stone speed indicators, one driven from the bogie and the other from the rear driving wheel. The front one was fitted in May 1951 and then taken off in June 1954 at the same works visit as it was repainted from the well-worn blue livery seen in this photograph at Preston, into the then preferred green livery. **Both: Rail Online**

Looking much more respectable on arrival here at Crewe on 12 April 1962 in her crimson lake livery, although this would not always be the case in her later years either. Finally, her cabside warning stripe has since been painted in and she is once again filthy, this time running under the wires past one the many modified over bridges on the WCML, this one being near Lichfield during September 1964 days before withdrawal week ending 3 October. She would have been a great favourite had preservation saved her and a splendid epitaph to the great man, sadly she was sold to J. Cashmore for scrap at Great Bridge instead. **Photos: *Neville Stead Collection/The Transport Library & Rail Online***

The ugly runs of conduit for her electric lighting can be seen opposite along with the first style of numbering for the British Railways smokebox numberplates, as 46257 City of Salford passes Weaver Junction with an up express during 1949. She had been under construction during the months up to nationalisation and was released from Crewe Works on 19 May 1948. This second view shows again the continued unkempt state of her lined black livery on 23 August 1951, as she blasts away from Glasgow Central with a relief train to the Royal Scot, in the meantime she has now acquired the approved version of her smokebox number plate. *Photos: R.A. Whitfield & George C. Lander/both Rail Photoprints*

Left: In this view on 2 April 1956, 46257 City of Salford attracts attention at the head of the 7:15am from Plymouth to Paddington, the engine having earlier arrived at Old Oak Common from the London Midland Region on 23 January 1956. This unusual turn of events arose in that very chilly winter, after the Western Region's prestige King Class 4-6-0s' were discovered to have serious problems with their bogies that required immediate attention at Swindon Works. As a result, both, 46254 City of Stoke-on-Trent and 46257 City of Salford, were sent to Old Oak Common on loan. They were joined in turn at the beginning of February by two Princess Royals, 46207 Princess Arthur of Connaught and 46210 Princess Patricia, very soon the Kings were repaired in sufficient numbers to release the LMR engines, and they were returned back home once more before the end of the month. Unfortunately for Stanier's reputation 46210 Princess Patricia disgraced herself on 10 February when her firebox brick arch collapsed whilst she was working the down Cornish Riviera from Paddington to Plymouth, and she was held in Laira's running shed whilst replacement bricks were obtained from her home region, probably from Crewe. **Rail Online**

Opposite: She attracts attention once more on 7 April 1957, this time from the younger generation upon her arrival at the buffer stops and retarders at Euston. Aside from her brief jaunt on the Western Region 46257 City of Salford was allocated to 1B Camden for her first decade of service, before being based out of Carlisle for her final years, firstly from Upperby in September 1958 and finally from Kingmoor. Although she was to be seen sacked over nameless and in open storage at Upperby from the close of 1963 until the middle of March 1964. **Colour Rail**

It would be inevitable perhaps that the last built locomotive of the class, 46257 City of Salford with just sixteen years of service life would record the lowest mileage for the class, recorded variously in publications as 797,758 miles or 806,758 miles or 841,782 miles, the reason being is that officially the actual mileages stopped being recorded after 1959, with estimates applied for the years that followed. Our closing view shows 46257 City of Salford still as a 1B Camden based locomotive most likely in the summer of 1958 before her transfer north speeding through Bletchley.
Colour Rail